Introduction

In a Nutshell

Here are two ways to look at Emily Dickinson's life:

Old thinking: Emily Dickinson was a shy crazy lady who dressed all in white, never left the house, and secretly wrote nearly two thousand poems that nobody saw until she died.

New thinking: Emily Dickinson was a gifted poet who chose—for reasons she kept private—to stay at home, write quietly and yes, wear white.

What's the difference between these two narratives, whose facts are pretty much the same? For the first ninety years after Dickinson's death in 1886, the public perception of her was closer to the first version. Poor Emily Dickinson, the story used to go. Such a great poet; too bad she couldn't get along like a normal person.

Sometime in the 1970s, though (thanks largely to a fantastic biography by Dickinson scholar Richard B. Sewall), views on Dickinson's life started to change. Maybe it wasn't that the secret bard of Amherst didn't know how to act like a normal person. Maybe she just didn't want to. People who knew Emily Dickinson well during her lifetime recalled her as warm and funny, with an impish streak. The more this picture emerges, the less Dickinson seems like a victim of pathological shyness. Could Emily Dickinson have been . . . a rebel, living her life exactly the way she wanted to, no matter what anybody else thought?

From the moment her collected poems were published for the first time after her death, Dickinson has been hailed as one of the great American poets. Her language, rhythm, and punctuation are totally unique, as was her lifestyle. And what's more American than a person unafraid to go her own way?

Biography

Biography

In 1881, a new arrival to the town of Amherst, Massachusetts learned of "a lady whom people call the Myth. She has not been outside of her own house in 15 years. She dresses wholly in white, and her mind is said to be perfectly wonderful. She writes finely, but no one ever sees her."[1] The Myth, of course, was Emily Dickinson.

There wasn't supposed to be anything mythical about Emily Dickinson's life. Born in 1839, the daughter of a prominent Massachusetts citizen, Dickinson would have been expected to receive a good education (for a woman, that is), to marry well, to raise children, and to spend her days tending to home and family.

As it turns out, Emily Dickinson did nothing by the rules. What's more intriguing, she arguably

made her greatest statements at times when she said nothing. She politely yet firmly refused to be converted at her Christian women's college and, with equal politeness, declined all visitors and social invitations in her later years. By doing so, Emily Dickinson quietly made an impact on those around her. No one at the time knew that she was saving her words for the hundreds of poems she wrote privately in her room, refusing to release them for publication. "No American has conversed with his or her soul as Emily Dickinson did," the literary critic Herbert Leibowitz once said.[2] By listening to her own soul, Dickinson taught us something about ours. (We're still not really sure what the all-white clothes were about, though. That was just her thing.)

Emily Dickinson didn't live as she did because she didn't have the ability to do otherwise. She did it because she wanted to. In her letters she revealed herself to be witty, intelligent, even flirtatious. Having lost many of her loved ones to untimely death, perhaps Dickinson withdrew as a way of rejecting a world so full of pain. Who knows why she chose to cut herself off from the world? Dickinson had her reasons, and she kept them to herself. As she told us in her poems, the soul selects its own society. It just so happens that her soul found completeness in itself.

Childhood

Emily Elizabeth Dickinson was born 10 December 1830 in Amherst, Massachusetts. She was born into a prominent family, though not an especially wealthy one. The Dickinsons were one of those noble New England clans who took their children to church, educated them well, and went about the business of quietly building the young republic. Dickinson's paternal grandfather, Samuel Dickinson, founded Amherst College. Her father, Edward Dickinson, was a lawyer and treasurer of Amherst College, a Massachusetts state representative and senator, a member of the governor's cabinet, and a U.S. Congressman. From Emily's journals and letters, it seems that her mother, Emily Norcross Dickinson, had an aloof personality and possibly suffered from depression. Emily was closer to her father (who exacted a powerful influence on her) and to her older brother William Austin and her younger sister Lavinia.

Emily Dickinson was born (and eventually died) in The Homestead, her father's house in Amherst. In 1840, Emily and Lavinia both started school at Amherst Academy, a converted boys' boarding school located in their hometown. Always physically frail, Emily was frequently absent in her seven years at the academy due to illness. In April 1844, when she was just thirteen, Emily's second cousin and close friend, Sophia Holland, died of typhus. The young girl's death was devastating to Dickinson, and she recovered from the loss only slowly. Holland's was the first of many partings that hung like a cloud over Dickinson's life and her poetry. "Parting is all we know of heaven/ And all we know of hell,"[3] Dickinson later wrote.

In 1846, Amherst Academy got a new headmaster, a young twentysomething named Leonard Humphrey. Dickinson grew close to her new principal. It turned out that Humphrey was just the first of many older men to whom Emily Dickinson latched onto throughout her lifetime, developing a powerful teacher-pupil relationship (always with Dickinson filling the role of student). She called Humphrey "master," a title she would give to all of her older mentors throughout her life.

**Emily Dickinson
Shmoop Biography**

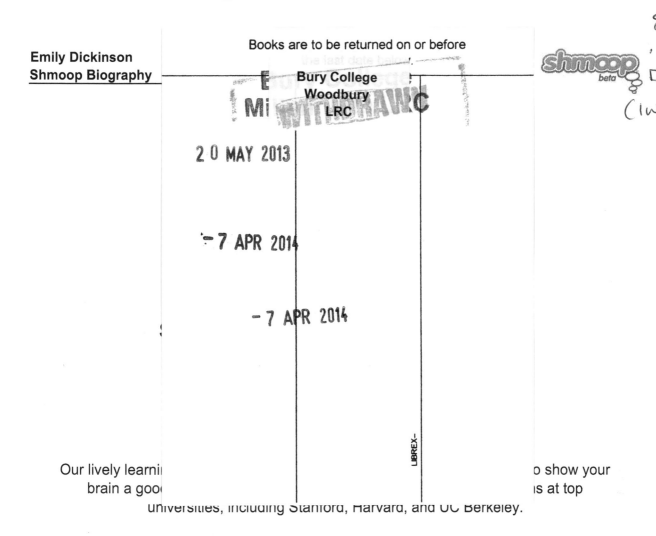
Our lively learni... ...o show your
brain a goo... ...s at top
universities, including Stanford, Harvard, and UC Berkeley.

Want more Shmoop? We cover literature, poetry, bestsellers, music, US history, civics,
biographies (and the list keeps growing). Drop by our website to see the latest.

www.shmoop.com

Table of Contents

Introduction 2
  In a Nutshell 2
Biography 2
  Biography 2
  Childhood 3
  Mount Holyoke & Amherst 4
  Poetry 4
  Recluse 5
  Death 6
Facts 6
  Trivia 6
  Family 7
Quotes 7
Resume 9
  Education 9
  Poems 9
Timeline 9
Best of the Web 13
  Books 13
  Websites 14
  Movies & TV 15
  Music 16
  Photos 17
  Video & Audio 17
  Primary Sources 18
Citations 19

Mount Holyoke & Amherst

After graduating from Amherst Academy in 1847, Dickinson enrolled at Mount Holyoke Female Seminary (now Mount Holyoke College). In her short time there, Dickinson stood out by refusing to take part in the school's Christian evangelical efforts. Dickinson held organized religion at arm's length all her life. She considered herself a believer, but never joined a church. "Some keep the Sabbath going to church," Dickinson wrote in a poem, "I keep it staying home."[4] This predilection was evident at Mount Holyoke. During one student assembly, headmistress Mary Lyon asked all students who wanted to be Christians to stand up. According to classmate Clara Newman Turner, only Dickinson remained seated. "They thought it queer I didn't rise. I thought a lie would be queerer," Newman Turner recalled Dickinson telling her.[5] Incidents like these are a pretty good indicator that Dickinson wasn't too happy at college. In the end, she lasted less than a year. On 25 March 1848, Emily's brother William Austin arrived at Mount Holyoke to escort her back to Amherst. She moved back into The Homestead and lived there for the rest of her life.

Dickinson's life in Amherst was not a particularly eventful one. "There are long periods of time—weeks, months, and on one occasion an entire year—for which not even the simplest quotidian activity of her routine can be ascertained,"[6] biographer Cynthia Griffin Wolff wrote, with more than a note of frustration. As the eldest unmarried daughter in her family, she was expected to care not only for her parents but also for her brother until he married in 1856. She did household chores, maintained the garden, and wrote poems privately in her spare time.

The most notable events in Dickinson's life were often tragic ones. In 1850, her former principal Leonard Humphrey died unexpectedly. "The tears come," Dickinson wrote to her old friend Abiah Root, "and I cannot brush them away; I would not if I could, for they are the only tribute I can pay the departed Humphrey."[7] By the mid-1850s, her mother had become bedridden with various illnesses that would plague her for the rest of her life. The burden of caring for her mother was great, and confined Dickinson to the house.

Poetry

Perhaps because of the mundane quality of her daily life, by the late 1850s Dickinson started taking her poetry more seriously. In 1858, she began the project of copying all of her previously written poems down into books. She also published a few poems around this time in the *Springfield Republican* newspaper, which was owned by family friend Samuel Bowles. Dickinson abhorred publishing, though, and only a handful of her poems were ever published during her lifetime.

In April 1862, literary critic and abolitionist Thomas Wentworth Higginson wrote an essay for *The Atlantic Monthly* addressed to aspiring writers. Soon after, Higginson received a letter postmarked from Amherst. "It was in a handwriting so peculiar that it seemed as if the writer might have taken her first lessons by studying the famous fossil bird-tracks in the museum of that college town,"[8] Higginson recalled. The letter read: "MR. HIGGINSON, - Are you too deeply occupied to say if my verse is alive? The mind is so near itself it cannot see distinctly, and I have none to ask. Should you think it breathed, and had you the leisure to tell me, I should feel

quick gratitude."9 Dickinson included four poems. "The impression of a wholly new and original poetic genius was as distinct on my mind at the first reading of these four poems as it is now," Higginson recalled.[10] He wrote back to Dickinson, beginning a correspondence and an unusual friendship that lasted to her death nearly 25 years later.

Higginson found himself mesmerized by his eccentric pen pal, who always addressed him as though he were her teacher, signing her letters "Your Scholar" or "Your Gnome" (which completely baffled Higginson). Her letters could be playful, even flirtatious. When Higginson asked for a photograph, she wrote back: "I had no portrait, now, but am small, like the wren; and my hair is bold, like the chestnut bur; and my eyes, like the sherry in the glass, that the guest leaves."[11] Five years after her death, Higginson still did not know what to make of his unusual friend. "The bee himself did not evade the schoolboy more than she evaded me," he wrote in 1891, "and even at this day I still stand somewhat bewildered, like the boy."[12]

Recluse

Higginson was not the only person who found Emily Dickinson elusive. By 1867, she had begun to withdraw from public life in ways her neighbors couldn't help but notice. She began speaking to callers only through the door, instead of face to face. She politely refused to meet company at The Homestead, retiring to her room instead when visitors called. Around this time, she also took to dressing exclusively in white dresses that she sewed herself. It wasn't that she was rude—she sent flowers or gifts in her place when she knew a visitor was coming. She spent time with her family and lavished attention on children, especially her nieces and nephews. She just preferred to be alone, thank you very much.

The Amherst social scene's loss was literature's gain. As Dickinson pulled away from society, her creative life blossomed. She wrote hundreds, even thousands of poems, all of which were dutifully copied down into the books. "In her astonishing body of 1,775 poems Dickinson records what is surely one of the most meticulous examinations of the phenomenon of human 'consciousness' ever undertaken," the novelist Joyce Carol Oates wrote.[13] Dickinson may not have known much of the outside world, but she knew herself completely.

Higginson traveled to Amherst to meet Dickinson for the first time in 1870—after the pair had been corresponding for eight years. "After a little delay, I heard an extremely faint and pattering footstep like that of a child, in the hall," he wrote of the meeting. "She came toward me with two day-lilies, which she put in a childlike way into my hand, saying softly, under her breath, 'These are my introduction,' and adding, also, under her breath, in childlike fashion, 'Forgive me if I am frightened; I never see strangers, and hardly know what I say.'" [14] Once she started talking, however, Dickinson wouldn't shut up. Higginson sat in stunned silence as Dickinson talked nonstop through their visit. "She seemed to speak absolutely for her own relief, and wholly without watching its effect on her hearer," he wrote. "She was much too enigmatical a being for me to solve in an hour's interview, and an instinct told me that the slightest attempt at direct cross-examination would make her withdraw into her shell; I could only sit still and watch, as one does in the woods."[15]

Dickinson didn't shut herself off completely from the world. In 1872 or 1873, she met and began writing to Massachusetts Supreme Court Judge Otis Phillips Lord. Some scholars believe their relationship turned romantic after the death of Lord's wife in 1877. Unfortunately, we can't know for sure. Lavinia Dickinson adhered to her sister's instructions to burn her letters after her death. Did Emily Dickinson ever have a boyfriend? Like so many things about her life, that remains a mystery.

Death

The last decade of Emily Dickinson's life was marked by death and loss. In 1874, her father Edward died of a stroke in Boston. Emily stayed upstairs in her room while the funeral service took place in the living room below. In 1882, her mother died. The year after that, her favorite nephew Gilbert died And the year after that, her friend and maybe-boyfriend Judge Lord died as well.

Soon it was the poet's turn. On 15 May 1886, after battling a kidney disease now known as nephritis, Emily Dickinson died at The Homestead, the house in which she was born. She was buried in a white dress, her casket carried across a field of buttercups before being laid to rest in Amherst's town cemetery. After her death, her sister Lavinia discovered the books that Emily had been carefully filling with poems—forty volumes, containing more than 800 poems. They were published for the first time in 1890 and have been wildly popular ever since.

Today we tend to see the color white as a symbol of virginity and innocence. Maybe we'd understand Emily Dickinson better if we remembered that she saw it as passion.

Dare you see a soul at the white heat?
Then crouch within the door;
Red is the fire's common tint,
But when the vivid ore

Has sated flame's conditions,
Its quivering substance plays
Without a color, but the light
Of unanointed blaze.[16]

Facts

Trivia

Edward Dickinson—Emily's father—went out in his underwear one night and woke up the entire town of Amherst with the church bells so that residents could see the northern lights.[17]

For a long time, it was believed that there was only one authenticated photograph of the adult Emily Dickinson. In 2000, Dickinson scholar Philip F. Gura found and purchased (on eBay!) a photograph that seemed to be a previously undiscovered portrait of the poet. Scholars are still debating whether the portrait actually is Emily Dickinson, though Gura's forensic analysis says

that it is.[18]

The epitaph on Emily Dickinson's grave reads simply, "Called Back." [19]

As an unmarried daughter, Dickinson was expected to handle chores around her parents' home. She willingly did the baking and the gardening, but balked at dusting and (not surprisingly) paying social visits.[20]

Was Emily Dickinson depressed or even suicidal? It is possible. In one of her letters to Thomas Wentworth Higginson, she wrote, "Of our greatest acts we are ignorant. You were not aware that you saved my life."[21]

Whenever she was asked why her sister chose to shut herself off from society, Lavinia Dickinson responded, "It was only a happen."[22]

Family
Father: Edward Dickinson (1803-1874)
Mother: Emily Norcross Dickinson (1804-1882)
Brother: William Austin Dickinson (1829-1895)
Sister: Lavinia Norcross Dickinson (1833-1899)

Quotes

"A letter always feels to me like immortality because it is the mind alone without corporeal friend."
— Emily Dickinson to Thomas Wentworth Higginson [23]

"I had no monarch in my life, and cannot rule myself; and when I try to organize, my little force explodes and leaves me bare and charred."
— Emily Dickinson to Thomas Wentworth Higginson, about 1862 [24]

"The truth must dazzle gradually."— Emily Dickinson [25]

"How lonely this world is growing, something so desolate creeps over the spirit and we don't know its name, and it won't go away."
— Emily Dickinson, 1850 [26]

"Emily Dickinson asked no favors from the world and granted it none. The truth seems to be that, like Thoreau, she had certain private affairs to transact that were more important to her."
— Biographer Richard B. Sewall [27]

My life closed twice before its close;
It yet remains to see
If Immortality unveil
A third event to me,
So huge, so hopeless to conceive,
As these that twice befell.
Parting is all we know of heaven,
And all we need of hell.

— Emily Dickinson, "My life closed twice before its close" [28]

Hope is the thing with feathers
That perches in the soul,
And sings the tune without the words,
And never stops at all,

And sweetest in the gale is heard;
And sore must be the storm
That could abash the little bird
That kept so many warm.

I've heard it in the chillest land,
And on the strangest sea;
Yet, never, in extremity,
It asked a crumb of me.

— Emily Dickinson, "Hope is the thing with feathers" [29]

I heard a Fly buzz—when I died—
The Stillness in the Room
Was like the Stillness in the Air—
Between the Heaves of Storm —

The Eyes around—had wrung them dry—
And Breaths were gathering firm
For that last Onset—when the King
Be witnessed—in the Room —

I willed my Keepsakes—Signed away
What portions of me be
Assignable—and then it was
There interposed a Fly —

With Blue—uncertain stumbling Buzz—
Between the light—and me—
And then the Windows failed—and then
I could not see to see—

— Emily Dickinson, "I heard a fly buzz when I died" [30]

"I hope you're very careful working, eating and drinking when the heat is so great--there are temptations there which at home you are free from--beware the juicy fruits, and the cooling ades, and cordials, and do not eat *ice-cream*, it is so very *dangerous*."

— Emily Dickinson, in a letter to brother William Austin Dickinson [31]

Resume

Education
Amherst Academy (1840-1847)
Mount Holyoke Female Seminary (1847-1848)

Poems
(Dickinson wrote thousands of poems; these are among her best known)

"Because I could not stop for death"
"I heard a fly buzz when I died"
"Hope is the thing with feathers"
"My life closed twice before its close"
"I felt a Funeral, in my brain"
"The Soul selects her own society"
"There is no frigate like a book"
"There's a certain slant of light"
"I'm Nobody! Who are you?"
"Safe in their Alabaster chambers"

Timeline

December 10, 1830

Emily Dickinson Born
Emily Elizabeth Dickinson is born in Amherst, Massachusetts. She is the second of three children of Edward and Emily Norcross Dickinson.

September 7, 1840

School
Emily and her sister Lavinia begin classes at Amherst Academy, a converted boys' school. In her seven years of schooling there, she is frequently absent due to illness.

April 1844

Cousin Dies
Dickinson's second cousin and good friend Sophia Holland dies of typhus. Thirteen-year-old Emily is deeply shaken by the girl's death.

1846

Meets Leonard Humphrey
Leonard Humphrey, an educator in his early twenties, takes over as principal of Amherst Academy. Dickinson grows close to him as a friend and mentor. He is one of several older men she refers to throughout her life as a "master."

August 10, 1847

Mount Holyoke
Dickinson completes her studies at Amherst Academy and enrolls at the Mount Holyoke Female Seminary (later Mount Holyoke College). Mount Holyoke classifies its students into three religious categories: women who were "established Christians," women who "expressed hope," and those "without hope." Dickinson is a No Hoper.

March 25, 1848

Return to Amherst
Less than a year into college, Dickinson quits her studies for reasons that remain unclear—possibly poor health, homesickness, her parents' wishes or her dislike of the school. Her brother Austin arrives at Mount Holyoke to escort her home.

1850

Leonard Humphrey Dies
Dickinson's friend and former principal, Leonard Humphrey, dies unexpectedly at the age of 25. "The tears come, and I cannot brush them away; I would not if I could, for they are the only tribute I can pay the departed Humphrey," Dickinson writes to her friend Abiah Root.[32]

1855

Travels Outside Massachusetts

For the first and only time in her life, Dickinson travels outside the borders of her home state. With her mother and sister, she spends three weeks in Washington, D.C. visiting her Congressman father; she then spends two weeks with relatives in Philadelphia. After their return, Dickinson's mother falls ill.

1856

Marriage of William Dickinson and Susan Gilbert

Dickinson's brother, William, marries Emily's friend, Susan Gilbert. The new sisters-in-law have an intense, tempestuous relationship. Though Dickinson craves Gilbert's approval, the aloof, brooding Gilbert frequently hurts her delicate sister-in-law's feelings.

1858

Copies Poems

Dickinson starts making formal copies of her poems. Some of her verses appear in the *Springfield Republican*, a paper edited by her friend, Samuel Bowles.

April 1862

Literary Friendship

After reading an essay by literary critic and abolitionist Thomas Wentworth Higginson in *The Atlantic Monthly*, Dickinson writes him to ask him to review her poetry. They strike up a correspondence that lasts for years.

1864

Poems Published

Poems appear in *Drum Beat* to raise money for Union soldiers' medical expenses. Dickinson also publishes poems in the *Brooklyn Daily Union*.

1867

Isolation

Dickinson begins to voluntarily withdraw from social life, preferring to speak with visitors through a door rather than face-to-face. It is her most productive period of writing. She stays socially active by sending numerous letters to favorite correspondents.

1870

Meets Higginson

After repeatedly declining his requests for a meeting or photograph, Dickinson meets Thomas Wentworth Higginson, her pen pal of eight years. "She came toward me with two day-lilies, which she put in a childlike way into my hand, saying softly, under her breath, 'These are my introduction,'" Higginson recalled of their unusual meeting. [33]

1872

Meets Judge Otis

In 1872 (or possibly in 1873), Dickinson makes the acquaintance of Massachusetts Supreme Court Judge Otis Phillips Lord. They exchange numerous letters over the years. Scholars speculate that the two may have become romantically involved after the death of Otis's wife in 1877.

June 16, 1874

Father Dies

Dickinson's father, Edward, dies of a stroke in Boston at the age of 71. He is buried in Amherst. Emily Dickinson does not attend her father's services, listening to the funeral instead from her room upstairs.

November 14, 1882

Mother Dies

Dickinson's mother, Emily Norcross Dickinson, dies. Her death relieves Emily, who had spent much of the last 30 years caring for her bedridden mother.

1883

Nephew Dies

Gilbert Dickinson, William and Susan's son and Emily's favorite nephew, dies of typhoid fever.

March 1884

Judge Otis Dies

Dickinson's maybe-boyfriend, Judge Otis Phillips Lord, dies.

May 15, 1886

Emily Dickinson Dies

Emily Dickinson dies of Bright's Disease —a kidney ailment now known as nephritis. After her coffin is carried—per her instructions—through fields of buttercups, she is buried in West Cemetery in Amherst.

1890

Book of Poetry Published

Dickinson's sister, Lavinia, discovers hundreds of Emily's unpublished poems in her desk after her death. They are published together for the first time four years after Emily's death and become wildly successful, going through eleven printings in two years.

Best of the Web

Books

Emily Dickinson, *The Complete Poems of Emily Dickinson*
http://www.amazon.com/Complete-Poems-Emily-Dickinson/dp/0316184136/ref=sr_1_1?ie=UTF
8&s=books&qid=1253220017&sr=8-1
Dickinson abhorred the idea of releasing her poetry to the public, calling the act of publishing

"the auction of the mind."[34] After Dickinson died in 1886, her sister Lavinia discovered more than 800 poems neatly bound and copied in her bedroom. The collection of Emily Dickinson's poetry was published in 1890 and has been beloved since.

Martha Dickinson Bianchi, *The Life and Letters of Emily Dickinson* (1924)
http://www.amazon.com/Life-Letters-Emily-Dickinson/dp/B0015YHY1S/ref=sr_1_1?ie=UTF8&s=
books&qid=1253220048&sr=1-1
Dickinson's niece Martha published this biography of her aunt nearly 40 years after the poet's death. It is far from definitive, but offers an intimate portrait of an unusual woman, a woman

whose loved ones remembered as warm and funny.

Richard B. Sewall, *The Life of Emily Dickinson* (1974)
http://www.amazon.com/Life-Emily-Dickinson-Richard-Sewall/dp/0674530802/ref=sr_1_1?ie=U
TF8&s=books&qid=1253220075&sr=1-1
Sewall's biography is considered to be the definitive word on Dickinson's life, and no one has
surpassed it since. Prior to publication, Dickinson had acquired a reputation as a shy, fragile
woman unable to leave her house. Sewall's research showed that Emily Dickinson was a lot
smarter and pluckier than biographers had given her credit for.

Brenda Wineapple, *White Heat: The Friendship of Emily Dickinson and Thomas Wentworth
Higginson* (2008)
http://www.amazon.com/White-Heat-Friendship-Dickinson-Wentworth/dp/1400044014/ref=sr_1_
1?ie=UTF8&s=books&qid=1253220093&sr=1-1
In 1862, after reading his essay in the *Atlantic Monthly*, Dickinson wrote to literary critic Thomas
Wentworth Higginson to ask him to review her poetry. What followed was a fascinating, unusual
correspondence that lasted decades. In her letters, Dickinson showed herself to be intelligent,
sensitive, coquettish, and eccentric. This book looks at Dickinson's illuminating relationship with
a man she called her "master."

Websites
Dickinson Electronic Archives
http://www.emilydickinson.org/
The Dickinson Electronic Archives is an online center dedicated to Dickinson's work. It features
rare images of writing by Dickinson, her family and friends, as well as transcriptions of the faint,
hard-to-read 19th century script. Unfortunately, you have to have a password to access some
materials, but you can still find enough on here to sate your curiosity (or your research
requirements).

The Poetry Foundation
http://www.poetryfoundation.org/archive/poet.html?id=1775
The Poetry Foundation has a thorough, insightful biography of Dickinson, as well as links to her
poems. It also has a detailed reading list and bibliography to point you in the right direction if
you're doing an in-depth project.

Academy of American Poets
http://www.poets.org/poet.php/prmPID/155
The Academy is one of the best resources on the Web for poets and poetry. Dickinson's page
offers a biography, as well as links to her poems and critical essays about her. We like poet
Michael Ryan's essay on why Dickinson is his favorite poet.

Erin's Emily Dickinson Page
http://www.cswnet.com/~erin/emily.htm
Dickinson fan Erin has put together this swell website linking the best Dickinson-related sites
and articles on the Web. Some of the links are out of date, but she has some fun finds. She also
helpfully explains how to cite her page—don't plagiarize from her (or anyone)!

Emily Dickinson Museum
http://www.emilydickinsonmuseum.org/index.html
Dickinson spent almost her entire life in two homes in Amherst, Massachusetts: The
Homestead, where she was born and raised, and the Evergreens, the house next door where
her brother and sister-in-law lived. The two homes have now been turned into a museum
dedicated to honoring Dickinson's life and works.

Emily Dickinson Page, Brooklyn College
http://academic.brooklyn.cuny.edu/english/melani/cs6/dickinson.html
Associate professor Lilia Melani has put together a great Web component to her Brooklyn
College course on Emily Dickinson. Her page has information on Dickinson's biography and
poems, as well as some helpful instructions on how to read and analyze Dickinson's work.

Movies & TV

Angles of a Landscape (2008)
http://www.sawmillriver.com/videostore/emilydickinson.html
The Emily Dickinson Museum in Amherst, Massachusetts created this 32-minute documentary
about Dickinson's life. It focuses on the house in Amherst where Dickinson spent the vast
majority of her adult life. Known as The Homestead, Dickinson was born in the home and
gradually shut herself away within it as she became an adult.

Official Selection (2008)
http://www.officialselectionthefilm.com/Home.html
This short film is a spoof of pretentious short films. The film breaks down into three different
storylines—all parodies—two of which feature Emily Dickinson. We don't know if we're more
interested in the one about Dickinson and her "psycho-sexual visions of her past affairs" or the
one in which a present-day woman named Emily Dickinson "is trapped by the imperialist policy
of modern America war."

Loaded Gun: Life, and Death, and Dickinson (2002)
http://www.pbs.org/independentlens/loadedgun/
When filmmaker Jim Wolpaw embarked on a quest to find the "real" Emily Dickinson, he found
that the reclusive poet's nature eluded him. After exhausting the typical routes of a
documentary filmmaker—biographers, historians, and such—he holds a "casting call" for a
Hollywood-type film of Dickinson's life. The documentary takes an unusual turn from there.

Voices and Visions: Emily Dickinson (1999)
http://www.amazon.com/Voices-Visions-Emily-Dickinson-VHS/dp/1572527994
This entry in the celebrated documentary series looks at Emily Dickinson. The documentary is
noteworthy for the famous writers who are commentators, such as Adrienne Rich and Joyce
Carol Oates.

Beauty Crowds Me (1998)
http://www.imdb.com/title/tt0168497/
This award-winning, Canadian short film is based on the poetry of Emily Dickinson. It made the
rounds of the film festival circuit about ten years ago, but might be hard to find now.

Emily Dickinson: A Certain Slant of Light (1978)
http://www.amazon.com/Emily-Dickinson-Certain-Slant-Light/dp/B000F9RLQM
Acclaimed actress and Dickinson devotee Julie Harris narrates this documentary about the poet's life. Harris leads viewers through Dickinson-related sites in Amherst, Massachusetts, where she spent nearly all of her life.

Music

Aaron Copland
http://www.poets.org/viewmedia.php/prmMID/5799
The Pulitzer Prize-winning American composer Aaron Copland—composer of songs such as *Fanfare for the Common Man*—was a big fan of Emily Dickinson's. He created vocal and piano arrangements for twelve of Dickinson's poems. The first was performed in 1950.

Leo Smit, *The Ecstatic Pilgrimage*
http://library.buffalo.edu/music/exhibits/smit/
When the American composer, musician, and educator Leo Smit read the works of Emily Dickinson, he declared that he had found "a soulmate who answered my emotional needs and stimulated my musical desires."[35] Already a fan of Aaron Copland's arrangement of her poems, Smit composed six song cycles referencing more than 80 of Dickinson's poems, together known as *The Ecstatic Pilgrimage*.

Ernst Bacon
http://www.ernstbacon.org/index.htm
Ernst Bacon was an American composer who often turned to the nation's great poets for inspiration. Emily Dickinson was an obvious choice. Bacon set several Dickinson poems to music, as well as excerpts from her diary.

Jules Langert, *Three Emily Dickinson Songs*
http://www.recmusic.org/lieder/assemble_texts.html?SongCycleId=112
Composer Jules Langert created a song cycle based on three Emily Dickinson poems. The poems are "Much Madness Is Divinest Sense," "The Spider Holds a Silver Ball," and "The Heart Asks Pleasure First."

Jay Anthony Gach, *Letter to Abiah*
http://www.sibeliusmusic.com/index.php?sm=home.score&scoreID=72065
This arrangement for voice and piano was inspired by a letter that Dickinson wrote to her childhood friend Abiah Root in 1850. The young women traded many letters over the years.

Michael Gordon, *Lightning At Our Feet*
http://www.nytimes.com/2008/12/11/arts/music/11ligh.html
Artist Michael Gordon composed this multimedia work in homage to Emily Dickinson. It includes vocal performances of poems such as "The Soul Selects Her Own Society," as well as chamber music and visual dramatics.

Photos

Emily Dickinson
http://upload.wikimedia.org/wikipedia/commons/3/38/Black-white_photograph_of_Emily_Dickins
on2.jpg
The only confirmed portrait of Dickinson in adulthood, taken while she was a student at Mount
Holyoke.

Young Dickinson
http://upload.wikimedia.org/wikipedia/commons/f/f3/EmilyDickinson-drawing.jpg
A drawing of Emily Dickinson, age nine.

Maybe Dickinson?
http://www.writespirit.net/authors/emily_dickinson/Emily%20Dickinson.JPG
An unauthenticated portrait rumored to depict a young Dickinson.

The Homestead
http://culture-h.jp/hatadake-katsuyo-english/photo/EmilyDickinson.jpg
The Amherst house where Dickinson lived all of her life. It is now the Emily Dickinson Museum.

Dickinson's room
http://blog.syracuse.com/shelflife/dickinsonroom.jpg
Emily Dickinson's bedroom at The Homestead.

Dickinson's Grave
http://zhurnaly.com/images/zhurnalnet_z_images/emily_dickinson.jpg
Her burial site in Amherst, Massachusetts.

Dickinson Tattoo
http://www.pbs.org/independentlens/loadedgun/images/phFilm3.jpg
The ink on Dickinson fan Phillip Jenks's back. We don't recommend this, to be honest.

Video & Audio

Dickinson Readings
http://town.hall.org/Archives/radio/IMS/HarperAudio/012794_harp_ITH.html
Dickinson's poetry read by actress Julie Harris.

"Because I Could Not Stop for Death"—Rap
http://www.youtube.com/watch?v=jwVZtT9uDNM
Ashley Steeckel, Kelsey Larsen, and Casey Riley made this rap video for their AP Literature
class. And we love it.

"Because I Could Not Stop for Death"—Chamber Music
http://www.youtube.com/watch?v=ousRlAGZ_50&feature=related
Charles Jason Bechtold composed the musical arrangement of Dickinson's poem.

"I Heard a Fly Buzz When I Died"

http://www.youtube.com/watch?v=DzK0mQER28A&feature=related
A beautifully animated version of the poem.

"Ample Make This Bed"
http://www.youtube.com/watch?v=uGeqdYTaZbs&feature=fvw
A Dickinson poem read in the film *Sophie's Choice* .

Dickinson's Grave
http://www.youtube.com/watch?v=AS0Smx-ZCO0
No cash for a ticket to Amherst? The Springfield Intruder shares his trip to her gravesite.

Primary Sources

The Complete Poems
http://www.bartleby.com/113/
Text of the 1924 edition of Dickinson's poetry, with a foreword by her niece.

Dickinson's Obituary
http://www.venexia.com/clarkcon/dickinson3.html
The 1886 obit in the Springfield Republican, written by her sister in law Susan Dickinson.

Emily Dickinson's Letters
http://www.theatlantic.com/unbound/poetry/emilyd/edletter.htm
An essay Thomas Wentworth Higginson wrote about his correspondence with Dickinson, published in 1891 after her death five years earlier.

Letter to a Young Contributor
http://www.emilydickinson.org/higgyc/yct1.html
Higginson's 1862 essay that sparked the correspondence between Higginson and Dickinson.

Higginson Letter
http://www.gdn.edu/Faculty/cperkowski/dickinson/second%20letter.jpg
Image of a letter Dickinson wrote to Thomas Wentworth Higginson.

"Wild Nights"
http://upload.wikimedia.org/wikipedia/commons/b/be/Emily_Dickinson_%22Wild_nights%22_ma
nuscript.jpg
The manuscript of Dickinson's poem in her own handwriting.

"A Route of Evanescence"
http://upload.wikimedia.org/wikipedia/commons/d/df/Emily_Dickinson´s_(1830-1886)_manuscrip
t_of_%22A_route_of_evanescence%22_(1880).jpg
The original manuscript of the poem.

"Soul at the White Heat"
http://www.usfca.edu/fac-staff/southerr/romance.html
A 1987 critical essay on Dickinson by novelist Joyce Carol Oates.

Citations

[1] Richard Sewall, The Life of Emily Dickinson, http://books.google.com/books?id=odjlKZKYHJQC&printsec=frontcover&dq=The+life+of+emily+dickinson#v=onepage&q=&f=false, Accessed 25 August 2009.

[2] Thomas Wentworth Higginson, "Emily Dickinson's Letters," The Atlantic, October 1891, http://www.theatlantic.com/unbound/poetry/emilyd/edletter.htm, Accessed 25 August 2009.

[3] Holland Cotter, "Critic's Notebook: Sights Trained Yet Again on Amherst's Elusive Belle," New York Times, 14 October 1999, http://www.nytimes.com/1999/10/14/books/critic-s-notebook-sights-trained-yet-again-on-amherst-s-elusive-belle.html, Accessed 24 August 2009.

[4] Herbert Leibowitz, "The Life of Emily Dickinson," New York Times, 22 December 1974, http://topics.nytimes.com/top/reference/timestopics/people/d/emily_dickinson/index.html?scp=1-spot&sq=emily%20dickinson&st=cse, Accessed 24 August 2009.

[5] Emily Dickinson, "My life closed twice before its close," http://academic.brooklyn.cuny.edu/english/melani/cs6/closed.html, Accessed 28 August 2009.

[6] Emily Dickinson, "Some keep the Sabbath going to church," Bartleby, http://www1.bartleby.com/113/2057.html, Accessed 28 August 2009.

[7] "Emily Dickinson," The Poetry Foundation, http://www.poetryfoundation.org/archive/poet.html?id=1775, Accessed 25 August 2009.

[8] Michiko Kakutani, "Books of the Times," New York Times, 12 November 1986, http://www.nytimes.com/1986/11/12/books/books-of-the-times-275986.html, Accessde 25 August 2009.

[9] Richard Sewall, The Life of Emily Dickinson, http://books.google.com/books?id=odjlKZKYHJQC&printsec=frontcover&dq=The+life+of+emily+dickinson#v=onepage&q=&f=false, Accessed 25 August 2009.

[10] Thomas Wentworth Higginson, "Emily Dickinson's Letters," The Atlantic, October 1891, http://www.theatlantic.com/unbound/poetry/emilyd/edletter.htm, Accessed 25 August 2009.

[11] Thomas Wentworth Higginson, "Emily Dickinson's Letters," The Atlantic, October 1891, http://www.theatlantic.com/unbound/poetry/emilyd/edletter.htm, Accessed 25 August 2009.

[12] Thomas Wentworth Higginson, "Emily Dickinson's Letters," The Atlantic, October 1891, http://www.theatlantic.com/unbound/poetry/emilyd/edletter.htm, Accessed 25 August 2009.

[13] Thomas Wentworth Higginson, "Emily Dickinson's Letters," The Atlantic, October 1891, http://www.theatlantic.com/unbound/poetry/emilyd/edletter.htm, Accessed 25 August 2009.

[14] Thomas Wentworth Higginson, "Emily Dickinson's Letters," The Atlantic, October 1891, http://www.theatlantic.com/unbound/poetry/emilyd/edletter.htm, Accessed 25 August 2009.

[15] Joyce Carol Oates, "'Soul at the White Heat': The Romance of Emily Dickinson's Poetry," Critical Inquiry, Summer 1987, http://www.usfca.edu/fac-staff/southerr/romance.html, Accessed 28 August 2009.

[16] Thomas Wentworth Higginson, "Emily Dickinson's Letters," The Atlantic, October 1891, http://www.theatlantic.com/unbound/poetry/emilyd/edletter.htm, Accessed 25 August 2009.

[17] Thomas Wentworth Higginson, "Emily Dickinson's Letters," The Atlantic, October 1891, http://www.theatlantic.com/unbound/poetry/emilyd/edletter.htm, Accessed 25 August 2009.

[18] Emily Dickinson, "Dare you see a soul at the white heat," Bartleby, http://bartleby.com/113/1033.html, Accessed 28 August 2009.

[19] Renee Tursi, "The Self Containment Artist," New York Times, 21 October 2001, http://www.nytimes.com/2001/10/21/books/the-self-containment-artist.html, Accessed 24 August 2009.

[20] Philip F. Gura, "How I Met and Dated Miss Emily Dickinson," Common-Place, http://www.common-place.org/vol-04/no-02/gura/, Accessed 28 August 2009.

[21] Thomas Hampson, "Emily Dickinson," I Hear America Singing, PBS, http://www.pbs.org/wnet/ihas/poet/dickinson.html, Accessed 28 August 2009.

[22] "Emily Dickinson," The Poetry Foundation, http://www.poetryfoundation.org/archive/poet.html?id=1775, Accessed 25 August 2009.

[23] Thomas Wentworth Higginson, "Emily Dickinson's Letters," The Atlantic, October 1891, http://www.theatlantic.com/unbound/poetry/emilyd/edletter.htm, Accessed 25 August 2009.

[24] Herbert Leibowitz, "The Life of Emily Dickinson," New York Times, 22 December 1974, http://topics.nytimes.com/top/reference/timestopics/people/d/emily_dickinson/index.html?scp=1-spot&sq=emily%20dickinson&st=cse, Accessed 24 August 2009.

[25] Thomas Wentworth Higginson, "Emily Dickinson's Letters," The Atlantic, October 1891, http://www.theatlantic.com/unbound/poetry/emilyd/edletter.htm, Accessed 25 August 2009.

[26] Thomas Wentworth Higginson, "Emily Dickinson's Letters," The Atlantic, October 1891, http://www.theatlantic.com/unbound/poetry/emilyd/edletter.htm, Accessed 25 August 2009.

[27] Holland Cotter, "Critic's Notebook: Sights Trained Yet Again on Amherst's Elusive Belle," New York Times, 14 October 1999, http://www.nytimes.com/1999/10/14/books/critic-s-notebook-sights-trained-yet-again-on-amherst-s-elusive-belle.html, Accessed 24 August 2009.

[28] Renee Tursi, "The Self Containment Artist," New York Times, 21 October 2001, http://www.nytimes.com/2001/10/21/books/the-self-containment-artist.html, Accessed 24 August 2009.

[29] Herbert Leibowitz, "The Life of Emily Dickinson," New York Times, 22 December 1974, http://topics.nytimes.com/top/reference/timestopics/people/d/emily_dickinson/index.html?scp=1-spot&sq=emily%20dickinson&st=cse, Accessed 24 August 2009.

[30] Emily Dickinson, "My life closed twice before its close," http://academic.brooklyn.cuny.edu/english/melani/cs6/closed.html, Accessed 28 August 2009.

[31] Emily Dickinson, "Hope is the thing with feathers," Poets.org, http://www.poets.org/viewmedia.php/prmMID/19729, Accessed 28 August 2009.

[32] Emily Dickinson, "I heard a fly buzz when I died," Poets.org, http://www.poets.org/viewmedia.php/prmMID/15393, Accessed 28 August 2009.

33 "Emily Dickinson," The Poetry Foundation,
http://www.poetryfoundation.org/archive/poet.html?id=1775, Accessed 25 August 2009.

34 Holland Cotter, "Critic's Notebook: Sights Trained Yet Again on Amherst's Elusive Belle,"
New York Times, 14 October 1999,
http://www.nytimes.com/1999/10/14/books/critic-s-notebook-sights-trained-yet-again-on-amherst-s-elusive-belle.html, Accessed 24 August 2009.

35 John Bewley, curator, "Remembering Leo Smit," University at Buffalo Music Library,
http://library.buffalo.edu/music/exhibits/smit/, Accessed 26 August 2009.